Praye

and Poems

for Children

Adaptations by
Sarah Toast

Illustrations by
Thomas Gianni

Interior art consultation by
David M. Howard, Jr., Ph.D.

Louis Weber, C.E.O.
Publications International, Ltd.
7373 North Cicero Avenue
Lincolnwood, Illinois 60646

Manufactured in U.S.A.

8 7 6 5 4 3 2 1

ISBN: 0-7853-2216-7

PUBLICATIONS INTERNATIONAL, LTD.
Rainbow is a trademark of Publications International, Ltd.

Thank you for the world so sweet,
Thank you for the food we eat.
Thank you for the birds that sing,
Thank you, God, for everything.

Dear Lord, teach this child to pray,
And then accept my prayer.
You hear all the words I say
For You are everywhere.

God is great,
And God is good.
Now we thank Him
For this food. Amen.

Thank you, O Lord,
For these, Thy gifts,
Which we are about to receive
From Thy bounty. Amen.

God be in my head

   And in my thinking.

God be in my eyes

   And in my seeing.

God be in my mouth

   And in my speaking.

God be in my heart

   And in my understanding.

To do to others as I would

That they should do to me

Will make me gentle, kind, and good,

As children ought to be.

God made the sun,
   And God made the trees.
God made the mountains,
   And God made me.

Thank you, O God,
   For the sun and the trees,
For making the mountains,
   And for making me.

I see the moon.
The moon sees me.
God bless the moon,
And God bless me.

All things bright and beautiful,
All creatures great and small,
All things wise and wonderful—
The Lord God made them all!

Each little flower that opens,
Each little bird that sings—
He made their glowing colors;
He made their tiny wings.

He gave us eyes to see them
And lips that we might tell
How great is God Almighty,
Who has made all things well!

Two little eyes to look to God,
Two little ears to hear His word.
Two little feet to walk in His ways,
Hands to serve Him all my days.

What can I give Him,
  Poor as I am?
If I were a shepherd,
  I would bring a lamb.
If I were a wise man,
  I would do my part.
But what can I give Him?
  I will give my heart.

Jesus, friend of little children,
  Be a friend to me.
Take my hand and ever keep me
  Close to Thee.

Teach me how to grow in goodness
  Daily, as I grow.
Thou hast been a child,
  And surely Thou dost know.

Never leave me nor forsake me,
  Ever be my friend,
For I need Thee from life's dawning
  To its end.

Sleep, my child, and peace attend thee
  All through the night.
Guardian angels God will send thee
  All through the night.

Soft the drowsy hours are creeping,
  Hill and vale in slumber sleeping,
While the moon her watch is keeping
  All through the night.

O'er thy spirit gently stealing,
  Visions of delight revealing,
Breathes a pure and holy feeling
  All through the night.

Our Father, who art in Heaven,

Hallowed be Thy name.

Thy kingdom come,

Thy will be done

On earth as it is in Heaven.

Give us this day our daily bread,

And forgive us our trespasses

As we forgive those

Who trespass against us.

Lead us not into temptation,

But deliver us from evil.

For Thine is the kingdom,

And the power,

And the glory forever. Amen.

Day is done.

Gone the sun

From the lake,

From the hills,

From the sky.

All is well,

Safely rest.

God is nigh.